My Gymnastics Class

By Margaret Clyne With Rachel Griffiths

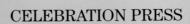

CELEBRATION PRESS
Pearson Learning Group

I went to gymnastics class.

There were many children.

First, we stretched.

Then we marched.

After that, I rolled on a mat.

I swung on a bar, too.

I learned a lot today!